THE YOUNG CITIZEN OBSERVES THE LAW

Authors

Albert H. Shuster, Ed.D.
Russell R. Miller, J.D.

Illustrated By
Lyn McClure Butrick

Editor
William H. Cooper, Ph.D.

University Classics, Ltd., Publishers
Athens, Ohio

Published by
University Classics, Ltd.
Athens, Ohio 45701

ii

Printing & Binding: The Lawhead Press, Inc.
Athens, Ohio 45701

Library of Congress Catalog Card Number: 83-080867

Printed in the United States of America

Contents

iii

Introduction

Our Society and the Law

Ours is a society of laws. Laws are the basic rules by which our everyday lives are governed. Our society depends upon laws in many ways. Nearly every part of each day and nearly everything we do is somehow affected by these laws—the regulation of traffic, the purity of our foods, the conditions of our work places. Thus, laws are necessary to ensure that our government and our society are orderly, safe, and healthful.

There are basically four sources of the laws that govern our society: (1) Constitutional Law, (2) Statutory Law, (3) Administrative Law, and (4) the Common Law.

The Constitutional Law is set forth in the United States Constitution and the Constitution of each of the several states. Each Constitution is a statement of basic laws and establishes the basic principles upon which all other laws must be based. The federal and state Constitutions set forth how the federal, state, and local governments are organized and the responsibilities of each of the branches of government. They state how, when, and how often the government officers (the President, State Governors, federal and state legislators, and judges) are elected.

The federal and state Constitutions guarantee all of us certain basic rights: the right to vote; the right to worship; the right of free speech; and the right to be treated equally under the law. No state can deny these rights. State Constitutions provide for more specific matters, such as the right to a free education that no school district can fail to provide, the right to a speedy trial, the establishment of legislative boundaries, and taxation.

The Statutory Law is that body of written law which has been adopted by the Congress of the United States or by the Legislatures of each of the several states. The Statutory Law is set forth in collections of the federal and state law usually called Codes. The Statutory Law addresses specific areas and problems which affect our lives and society.

Statutory Law further specifies how the federal, state, and local governments and courts are to be organized and operated. It sets forth those acts considered to be criminal acts and the punishment for them. It also governs marriage, divorce, and the custody of children whose parents are divorced. Statutory law also provides for the public health by establishing agencies to oversee the purity of our food and water, and public safety through the motor vehicle and job safety laws.

The Administrative Law consists of written rules and regulations adopted by various agencies of the government. The Administrative Law makes clear or adds information to the Statutory Law as it relates to each agency adopting the various rules and regulations.

Administrative rules and regulations have been adopted to govern the marking of public streets and highways to ensure safe driving. Regulations exist which set requirements on how food, water, and drugs (medicines) are prepared so that they are safe and healthful for consumption. Rules exist which define how buildings must be built in order to be sure that they are safe. Rules and regulations have even been adopted by administrative agencies to ensure that your school system operates properly to provide for you the education to which you have a right.

The Common Law is a large collection of legal rules which have been developed over time in decisions made by judges in various federal and state courts. The Common Law often interprets the Constitutional, Statutory, or Administrative Law; but the Common Law is also a separate body of law which governs our society and lives.

The Common Law is often the source of the law applied to resolve differences between and among the members of society. Common Law principles are applied in automobile accident cases to determine who is at fault. Persons' interests in property are also often based on the Common Law.

The law from each of these sources affects our everyday lives and governs the way we deal with each other on a day-to-day basis. It forms the rules by which we must live as members of society and it attempts to solve the problems that come about when rules are not followed.

There are people associated with each of these sources of law who either make the laws, administer the laws, or interpret the laws. These people are generally associated with one of the different parts, or branches, of our state and federal government. These branches of government are the Legislative Branch, the Executive Branch, and the Judicial Branch.

The most well-known members of the Legislative Branches—known as legislators—are the members of the United States Congress, Senators and Congressmen, State Legislators, and members of the local city councils. Legislators write and adopt the Statutory Law.

The most well-known members of the Executive Branches are the President of the United States, the governors of the several states, and the mayors of local cities, towns, and villages. Their basic responsibility is to see that Statutory and Administrative Law are put into practice and enforced in society. Your local policemen and firemen are among the most visible of the representatives of the Executive Branch.

Judges of the various levels of the federal, state, and city courts make up the Judicial Branch. Their responsibility is to interpret the laws, to apply those laws to conflicts that may arise between or among members of society, and to administer penalties—that is, fines or prison terms—to those who do not follow the laws.

We hope that, in using this book, you can learn about some of these laws and how they affect your relationships with others, as well as your responsibilities as a good citizen.

1 *A Trip to the Supermarket*

Roger and Peter had brought their model car kits over to Tim's house to work on in his father's basement shop. Answering the doorbell, Tim greeted them, "Hi, guys! I have to go to the store to get some things for my mother before we work on our models. Come along with me, will you?" They agreed to go with him, talking along the way about their projects.

As they were passing a bulk candy display at the store, Roger picked up a couple of jelly beans and popped them into his mouth.

"Hey, Rog, don't do that!" Tim protested. "That's stealing. If you got caught by one of the clerks, he could report you to the manager and you'd be in a lot of trouble."

Roger replied, "Aw, my mother always picks up a few grapes or cherries or something when she's at the fruit counter. I don't see anything wrong with that." Peter came into the discussion, "My mom does too. That's how she tells if she wants to buy some."

Tim stuck to his guns, "Well, my mother and father have taught me that taking even one piece of candy is no different from stealing money from the store—even a lot of money."

"Come on, Tim," Roger said, "the store will never miss that little bit. Besides, it's worth next to nothing."

"Sure," added Peter, "Roger's right. You wouldn't want to buy sour or rotten fruit, would you?"

"Pete, I think you're both wrong," Tim came back. "Do you think the manager would just get mad and chase you out of the store? My dad says you could be arrested for taking anything without paying for it—even one grape or cherry or peanut or piece of candy. Anyway, don't do it any more when you're with me."

The Law

Even such acts as shoplifting and eating food in a grocery store are dealt with by the Statutory law. In most states such acts are referred to as "theft offenses." The statute in one state is as follows:

(A) No person with purpose (intent) to deprive the owner of property or services, shall knowingly obtain or exert control over that person's property or services:
    (1) Without the consent of the owner of the property or services;
    (2) Beyond the scope of the express or implied consent of the owner or person authorized to give consent;
    (3) By deception; that is, by tricking the owner into giving up the property;
    (4) By threatening the owner to force him to give up the property;
(B) Whoever violates this section is guilty of theft. If the value of the property or services stolen is less than one hundred fifty dollars, a violation of the section is petty theft, a misdemeanor of the first degree. If the value of the property or services stolen is one hundred fifty dollars or more, a violation of this section is grand theft, a felony of the fourth degree.

2

Because shoplifting has become such a problem for merchants, many states have passed special statutes, such as the following ones, for dealing with shoplifters:

A merchant, or his employee or agent, who has probable cause (good reason) to believe that items offered for sale . . . have been unlawfully taken by a person, may . . . detain the person in a reasonable manner for a reasonable length of time within the (store) or its immediate vicinity.

The merchant or his employee or agent may detain another person for any of the following purposes:

(1) To recover the property unlawfully taken;
(2) To allow an arrest to be made by a peace officer;
(3) To obtain a warrant of arrest.

Discussion Questions

1. Do you agree with Tim or with Roger and Peter?
2. What do you think about Roger's argument that a few grapes or a couple of pieces of candy don't amount to anything in value?

3. Do you agree with Peter that a customer is justified in sampling fruit in order to see whether to buy some?
4. Is the law concerned only with the stealing of large items or money?
5. Is Tim's father right? Can you be arrested for taking anything in a store?
6. Talk this problem over with your mother and father and with your classmates.
7. Should Tim continue to associate with Roger and Peter?
8. What do you think about statutes like this? Do you think they are necessary?
9. The law draws a distinction between "petty" (small) and "grand" larceny; find out what the law is in your community.
10. A big supermarket may have up to several thousand customers per day; try to figure out the loss to the store if everybody took just a few grapes or cherries or something of the kind; how much money would be lost per day/week/month/year?
11. A bigger problem for stores is pilferage or shoplifting; is there any legal or moral difference between openly eating something in the store and putting something in your pocket without paying for it?
12. Commercial Services Systems (6946 Van Nuys Blvd., Van Nuys CA 91405) reports that about half of all customers "graze" or pilfer—at an average cost of $3.00 each and at a total annual national cost of over a billion dollars! Consider how much cheaper groceries and other goods could be if these losses were eliminated.

2 *The Neighbor's Car?*

Eleven-year old Jeff Walker had almost finished painting his bicycle bright red when his mother called him.

"I'll be there in a minute, Mom," he replied, "I want to finish this painting first."

But she insisted, "Come right now; I need you to run to the store to get some potatoes for supper. Your father will be home soon."

So Jeff went on the errand for his mother, leaving his brush lying across the top of the paint can.

It was about twenty minutes before he returned. When he got back, he noticed that there was less paint left than he had thought, but he finished painting his bicycle and put it in the garage to dry.

At the dinner table that evening, Jeff was telling his father about painting his bicycle when the doorbell rang. It was the next-door neighbor, Mr. Sloan, very upset. "I'm sorry to bother you at dinner time," he began, "but when I went out to get in my car, I found fresh red paint all over one side. It's the same color I saw Jeff out there painting his bike with. Now, why would he put that paint all over my new car?"

Jeff's mother invited Mr. Sloan to come in and called Jeff. When Jeff came into the living room, his mother asked him, "Jeff, did you put paint on Mr. Sloan's car?"

"No way," Jeff answered.

"But, Jeff," his mother added, "Mr. Sloan says it's the same color you used on your bike."

"Okay, Mom, but I didn't paint Mr. Sloan's car," Jeff replied.

"Now speak up, young man, and tell the truth," Mr. Sloan almost shouted.

"But I didn't paint your car," Jeff repeated.

"Well, then, I'll just have to call the police. They'll get the truth out of you."

Jeff was nearly in tears when his father entered the room, hearing Mr. Sloan's threat. Jeff's mother defended Jeff, saying, "Mr. Sloan, our son is not a liar." Mr. Walker added, "And I won't have you calling him one." He then turned to his son, "Jeff, who else was out there with you while you were painting your bike?"

"Nobody else, I was alone," Jeff admitted.

"Well, Jeff," said his father, "It looks bad for you if you were the only one using the paint."

Jeff's little five-year-old sister Patti, who had been listening from the kitchen, came running to her mother crying, "Are they going to put Jeff in jail?"

It was then that Mrs. Walker noticed the same red paint on Patti's dress. "Patti, did you put that paint on Mr. Sloan's car while Jeff was running that errand for me?" she asked.

Although she kept denying it, Patti cried louder and louder, but she finally got out, "Will they put me in jail if I did it?"

Mr. Walker took his daughter into his arms and calmed her down. Patti then confessed, "Jeff was painting his bike real pretty. I wanted Mr. Sloan's car to be pretty, too."

Mr. Walker assured Mr. Sloan that he had liability insurance and told him that he would arrange to have done whatever was necessary about the car—perhaps an auto paint shop could get the fresh paint off; or he might want to have the car repainted.

Mr. Sloan was not exactly happy with either of the solutions, since his car was less than a year old. He left still angry and upset. His last comment was, "People should look after their children."

The Law

In most states, young children like Patti would not themselves be liable or responsible for such an act because they are not old enough to be held legally responsible for their acts. That is, very young children are not considered to be capable of knowing right from wrong.

In some states the parents or other persons in charge of a child may be responsible for the acts of the child if the parent sees the child doing something it should not do and the parent does nothing to stop the child, or if the parent does not take reasonable steps to watch over the child.

Discussion Questions

1. Is Mr. Sloan right? Are Mr. and Mrs. Walker responsible for what their little daughter did? If so, why? If not, what different facts might make the Walkers responsible for Patti's actions?
2. Can Mr. Sloan sue Mr. Walker for a new car?
3. What is liability insurance?
4. Did Jeff have any responsibility for what his sister did?
5. What does the law where you live say about cases like this one?
6. Do you think Patti meant to hurt Mr. Walker's car? Does that make a difference?
7. Should Patti be punished for painting the neighbor's car? If not, why not? If yes, why? What form of punishment would you suggest?

7

3 *The Family Dog*

Buddy had found a new school friend whom he had visited only a few times before today. He told Chip that he would come over to play catch right after school, as soon as he had changed his clothes. Out of the house he ran and over to Chip's house he went. When he knocked on the door, Chip's mother called to tell Buddy that Chip would be right out. Buddy sat on the front steps to wait. Suddenly, Chip's dog, a big Irish setter, came running around the side of the house snapping and barking furiously.

As Trixie came running up the steps at him, Buddy drew back against the porch railing, about the same time that Chip opened the door and shouted, "Trixie, stay." Trixie stopped in her tracks and Chip said to Buddy, "Don't worry, she won't bite you." Buddy liked dogs and Trixie had never done this to him before. But each time he moved or tried to be friends, Trixie would bark until Chip would quiet her.

The two boys went to the side yard and began playing catch. Chip asked Buddy "How do you like my new first baseman's mitt?" Buddy looked at it admiringly and said, "I think it's neat! Can I try it for a while?" The two boys exchanged mitts and continued playing catch. Buddy liked the glove so much he called to Chip, "I'm going to ask my dad to get me one for my birthday."

Then Chip accidentally threw the ball over Buddy's head. As he ran to get the ball, Trixie came leaping toward him. He stopped in his tracks as he heard Trixie barking and coming upon him. Chip shouted at Trixie, but she kept running toward Buddy. She jumped on him and knocked him down and left teeth marks in his arm and ripped a hole in his jacket before Chip could grab her. Chip then took Trixie by the collar and chained her to the dog house.

Buddy said he felt O.K., so they went on playing catch until Buddy's mother called him for dinner. He told Chip he would see him later and he went home.

Buddy's mother noticed the ripped sleeve on his jacket and asked how it happened. As he was removing his jacket, she also noticed some blood and saw the marks on his arm. Buddy related the story about their playing catch and how Trixie had chased him when he missed the ball. She called Buddy's father from the living room where he was reading the paper and asked him to look at Buddy's arm. When Buddy told him what had happened, he insisted that they take Buddy to the emergency room at Riverside Hospital.

After the doctor treated Buddy's arm, he told them to contact Chip's parents and suggest that they keep the dog penned up for three weeks and to watch his behavior carefully. If the dog should become sick or die, they should rush Buddy to the hospital. Chip's parents were quite upset when Buddy's father called them and asked him to keep Trixie penned up all that time. Chip's mother said, "It must have been Buddy's fault that Trixie went after him. He must have been teasing her." Nevertheless, she said that she would keep the dog penned up.

Just a few days later the dog was loose and Buddy's mother called and told Chip's mother that Trixie was running around the neighborhood. Chip's mother replied that she had turned Trixie loose to get some exercise; she continued, "I don't plan to keep her penned up any longer. Anyway," she added, "it was all Buddy's fault, as he was on our property and the dog thought that she was protecting her own home."

The Law

The Common law of most states holds that animals and pets, like Chip's dog Trixie, are entitled to be "wild" one time. But if an animal has repeatedly shown that it is wild or vicious, its owner is responsible for the actions of the animal and is liable to anyone hurt by the animal.

Most cities and villages have passed specific statutory laws, or ordinances, to try to prevent situations like Buddy's. A violation of such ordinances is usually a criminal offense. One such ordinance is as follows:

No owner or keeper of any dog shall permit such dog to run at large, or allow any such dog off the premises (property) of the owner or keeper, unless such dog is restrained by a substantial (strong) leash, and any dog within the limits of the City must be restricted upon the premises of the owner or keeper by means of a secured fastening or suita-

ble enclosure, except that no leash shall be required
when a dog is under the supervision or control of
the owner or handler.

Discussion Questions

1. What does the law where you live say about this kind of
   problem?
2. How can you find out about how a law affects persons
   visiting friends?
3. What if Buddy got rabies? Do you know what this disease
   is?
4. What should good friends do about problems like this?

4 *The Picnic Panic*

Bobby White was on his way to a picnic at the lake outside town with Jerry Roberts and his parents. Both of the boys had been looking forward to this day ever since the plans had been made. They had hoped to fish in the morning and swim in the afternoon, but Mrs. Roberts had said no to the swimming; it was too early in the year and the water would be too cold.

"Okay, mom," Jerry had agreed, "We'll just fish twice as long and catch twice the fish."

Now, finally on their way, they could hardly wait to get there.

"I'll catch the first fish, Bobby," Jerry challenged. "Maybe so, Jerry, but I'll beat you by catching the most fish. And I'll also beat you in catching the biggest fish," Bobby answered.

When they arrived at the lake, it didn't take the boys long to pick out a picnic table up the hill, overlooking the lake and under a large tree. The station wagon was unloaded, Mr. Roberts settled into the folding chair which he had brought and began to read the morning paper, and Mrs. Roberts went about the final preparations for the picnic lunch.

Jerry and Bobby were eager to get in a little fishing before lunch.

"Come on, Bob, let's see how fast we can get our fishing gear rigged and in the water," Jerry urged his friend. Bobby was already on the move before Jerry finished speaking. They grabbed their poles, tied on the lures, and down the hill they raced, slipping and sliding on the wet grass, getting to the edge of the lake in a dead heat.

On his very first cast, Jerry got a strike. "Oh, boy, I told you I would catch the first one," he shouted, but it turned out to be a very small bluegill when he got it to shore.

"Jer, I use fish like that for bait," Bobby kidded him.

In a little while each of the boys had caught several fish, all of them quite small bluegills, though Bobby had the largest so far, so they were now tied in their challenges.

Watching some boats going by, out on the lake, Bobby said, "I sure wish we had a boat so we could go out where the big ones are."

"Well, why don't we fish off the back of one of these boats tied up on the shore?" asked Jerry. "That will put us a little farther out into deeper water. Maybe we can even catch some big bass."

Bobby replied, "I don't think we should. The owner might come and we'd be in trouble. It's probably against the law, just like going into somebody's house when there's nobody home."

But Jerry jumped from the bank into one of the boats. He landed on the front seat and a loud cracking noise was heard as his foot went clear through the fiberglass seat.

"Come on, let's get out of here," Jerry shouted to Bobby, jumping back out of the boat. They ran back to where they had first been fishing, trying to act as though they'd never left.

"Don't you think you'd better tell your dad what happened?" asked Bobby.

"No, and don't you say anything about it or my dad won't take us fishing again," Jerry responded. "Now remember, don't say anything at all." He was trying to pretend that he didn't care, but he was just as worried as Bobby.

Soon they were called for lunch, but neither of the boys felt much like eating. They took only small portions of the potato salad, just a small piece of chicken, ignored the celery and carrot sticks, and even refused dessert later.

"What's the matter, boys," laughed Mr. Roberts, "didn't catching all those big fish work up an appetite? You haven't eaten enough to feed the smallest one."

"I think I'm getting a headache," said Bobby.

"I've got kind of a stomach-ache," said Jerry.

After lunch the boys said they didn't feel like fishing any more. Mr. Roberts tried to get them interested in passing a football, a four-cornered frisbee-toss, and then a walk along the lakefront. But it was clear that the picnic had somehow been spoiled for the boys, so they decided to head back to town earlier than they had planned.

As they were packing up to go, Bobby said to Jerry, "I still think we should tell your dad what happened to the boat. After all, it was just an accident, wasn't it?"

But Jerry wouldn't budge. "No way, Bobby. We just can't. Now let's try to forget it. No one will ever know."

When they dropped him off, Bobby thanked Mr. and Mrs. Roberts, said so-long to Jerry, and ran into his house. He called out to his mother that he was home, went to his room, turned on the radio, and lay down on his bed. He couldn't get the boat incident out of his mind, but he finally dozed off and didn't wake up until his mother called him for dinner.

Again, he couldn't eat much.

Mr. White said, "Son, I can see that something is bothering you. Tell me what it is."

Bobby sobbed, "I'm afraid to tell you."

His father said, "Bobby, we've always been able to work things out, haven't we? Let's talk about it."

So Bobby told the whole story about what had happened to the boat.

"Did Jerry tell his dad?" his father asked.

"No," replied Bobby, "that's what's worrying me. I said we should, but Jerry wouldn't let me say anything."

"Well, we're going to talk to Mr. Roberts about this," Mr. White decided.

"Oh, no, Dad," Bobby begged, "Jerry will be mad at me if we do that."

"But shouldn't we be honest about it?" asked his father. "Just think how the owner is going to feel when he sees that broken seat in his boat. The damage has to be paid for."

Mr. White phoned Mr. Roberts and arranged for Bobby and him to meet that evening with Jerry and his father. Bobby was still somewhat worried; but he began to feel a little bit better, because now at least things were going to get settled.

The Law

Many states recognize in their Common Law some form of what is known as a "trespass" upon personal property. Personal property is property other than land. It consists of the moveable things we all own. A "trespass" is an entry upon the property, or rights to property, of another without the consent of the other. When a person commits a trespass upon the property of another, he is responsible for any damages which he may cause.

Because in most states a child is not considered capable of the intent, or purpose of mind, to commit a trespass, and thus be responsible for any damages he may cause, many states have enacted statutes making the child's parents responsible for the child's actions. The parents' responsibility is usually limited to the child's "willful" actions. Willful actions are actions done intentionally, with a mean purpose to cause damage.

Discussion Questions

1. Do you think Bobby and Jerry committed a trespass? Why or why not?
2. Were Bobby's and Jerry's actions "willful"? Why or why not?
3. Should Bobby's and Jerry's parents pay for the damage to the boat? Do you think that they should be required to?
4. Do Bobby's and Jerry's parents have any responsibility to watch over, or supervise, Bobby and Jerry? Why or why not?
5. Should Bobby and his parents, alone, pay for the damage? Why or why not?
6. What would you have done in Bobby's situation?
7. Can you recall anything happening to you that was like what happened to Jerry and Bobby? Did you ever break anything or destroy something that didn't belong to you and not tell the owner? Did Bobby and Jerry do what most people would do if they broke the seat in someone's boat and no one was around?
8. Why do you think this event bothered Bobby more than it bothered Jerry?
9. Would you have told Jerry's mother and father if you were Bobby? Why wouldn't you tell them? Or why would you tell them when Jerry told Bobby not to say anthing to his father?
10. Do you have any reason to believe that Jerry's father would have been any different from Bobby's father, if Jerry had told him? After all, it was an accident, wasn't it?

11. Do you think there is any difference between this kind
    of accident and one that occurs on the parking lot at the
    local shopping center when someone backs a car into
    another car and breaks the headlight? What should the
    driver do in this case? What should Jerry and Bobby
    have done about their accident?

17

5 *Velocipedes*

("Velocipede" is an old word for bicycle; Velocity = speed, ped/pedal = foot)

"Come on, you guys, it's time to hit the road," Michael announced to Jason and his sister Jessica. The three of them were off on a bike ride to downtown, and they had been looking forward to making a fun time of it.

"Let's race to see who can reach the stop sign first," Michael challenged them.

"Not me," said Jessica, "it's Saturday afternoon and there's too much traffic. There'll be a lot of people downtown, too. We'd better be extra careful today."

"Aw, Jessica, that's silly," Michael shot back, "you always make such a big deal of everything. People always watch out for kids on bikes. Well, come on, Jason, I'll beat you, anyway."

"I'll catch up later," said Jessica.

Jason didn't accept the challenge, either. As Michael took off in his wild and reckless way, Jason followed more cautiously, Jessica bringing up the rear.

When they arrived downtown, Jason observed, "Boy, you were right, Jessica. There sure are a lot of people down here today."

"Don't worry yourselves about it," Michael teased them. "Follow me!" He began pumping faster and faster, dodging between cars and weaving in and out of traffic.

"Michael, you shouldn't ride like that," Jessica called ahead to him. Then she screamed, "Michael, look out!" as a car changed lanes just as Michael started to pass it.

Luckily, Michael too saw in time what was happening and skidded his bike to a stop without being hit; but he and his bike went down, causing the car coming up behind him to have to come to a screeching stop as Michael scrambled to the side of the street, dragging his bike along with him.

"Golly, that was a little too close for comfort," Michael admitted to Jason and Jessica when they came up to him, soon relieved to learn that there was no serious damage to either Michael or his bike. A little shaken, though, Michael suggested "Maybe we'd better ride on the sidewalk from here on."

"I don't think we should do that, either," said Jessica. "Just look at all the people."

"Boy, Jessica, you're such a scaredy-cat," Michael told her, again putting on a brave front. "What do you want us to do, anyway, park our bikes and walk?"

"Maybe Jessica is right this time, Mike," Jason suggested. "There are a lot of people and the sidewalks are too crowded for bikes."

Michael was, by this time, his old self again: "I can't believe you guys. Are you coming or not?"

He jumped on his bike, hopped the curb, and began riding down the sidewalk. Jason and Jessica hesitated for a few moments, looking at each other with some doubt, then they got on their bikes and followed Michael.

They had not gone much farther before they came to even heavier pedestrian traffic. Michael was again going as fast as he dared, weaving around people as he rode. He called back over his shoulder, "Are you two ever going to catch up?" But just as he turned his head a lady stepped out of a store and started to cross the sidewalk in front of him.

"Michael, look out for that lady," Jessica warned at the top of her voice. Michael turned back quickly, but it was too late. He bumped into the lady, knocking her down, brushed by another lady with a young child, spilled a display stand outside the store, and crashed the front wheel of his bike through the glass door. Jason and Jessica jumped off their bikes. As Jason ran to Michael, Jessica hurried to help the woman up. "Are you all right?" Jessica inquired. "I guess so," she replied; then she shouted at Michael, "Young man, you could have hurt me badly. Don't you know the law about riding bicycles on the sidewalk?"

Jason in the meantime had helped Michael up and asked him if he was hurt. "No, I'm okay," said Michael, "just scared . . . and pretty ashamed of myself."

Fortunately, no one was seriously hurt in this accident. There was, however, some property damage to be settled later. And Jason and Jessica—and the crowd which gathered—were very upset with Michael.

"Next time I guess I'd better listen to what you and Jason have to say, Jessica," said Michael.

The Law

Riding bicycles recklessly—or even carefully—upon busy sidewalks can be dangerous. In an effort to prevent accidents like Michael's, most cities and villages have passed ordinances prohibiting reckless operation of a bicycle. One such ordinance is as follows:

No person shall operate a bicycle:

(a) Without regard for the safety and rights of pedestrians and as to endanger the life, limb, or property of any person while in the lawful use of the sidewalks or any public or private property.

(b) Without exercising reasonable and ordinary control over the bicycle.

(c) In a weaving or zigzag course unless it is necessary for safe operation in compliance with law.

(d) Without both hands upon the handle grips, except when necessary to give the required hand and arm signals.

(e) At a speed greater than is reasonable and prudent under the conditions at the time.

Because riding bicycles on sidewalks is especially dangerous, ordinances are often passed restricting that activity, as in the following ordinance:

(a) No person shall ride a bicycle upon a sidewalk within a business district.

(b) No person shall ride a motorized bicycle upon any sidewalk within the City.

(c) No person fifteen or more years of age shall ride a bicycle upon any sidewalk in any district.

(d) Whenever any person is riding a bicycle upon a sidewalk, he shall yield the right of way to any pedestrian and shall give audible signal before passing pedestrians.

Discussion Questions

1. What does it mean to "exercise reasonable and ordinary control" over a bicycle? Do you think Michael was doing so?

2. What does it mean to operate a bicycle at "reasonable and prudent speed under the conditions at the time?" Are there times when it is better to ride faster or slower than

at other times? When? Do you think Michael was following this ordinance?

3. Why does the second ordinance, above, make a distinction between a business district and other parts of the city?

4. Why do you think the second ordinance, above, makes a distinction between people fifteen years old and older and younger children? Why ought older persons be required to ride on the streets, rather than on the sidewalks?

5. Does your city have an ordinance like those above? Are they different? How?

6. What suggestions do you have for Michael, Jason, and Jessica about riding their bikes?

6 *Robert's Parents*

Jennifer had just arrived at the playground and started to play on the swings when she saw her friend Robert sitting against the fence in the corner of the playground. Vacation was almost over and Jennifer had not seen Robert all summer, so she ran over to speak to him. Jennifer noticed that he looked very sad.

"Hello, Robert," said Jennifer. "How has your summer been?" "Oh, hi, Jennifer," said Robert, "I guess it's been okay." "You don't look very happy," said Jennifer, "what's wrong?" "Aw, it's nothing," said Robert. "It sure doesn't seem like nothing to me," said Jennifer, "please tell me what's wrong."

"Well," said Robert, "It's my mom and dad. About three weeks ago my dad came home in the afternoon and had another argument with my mom. They really yelled a lot and dad packed his clothes and just left. I haven't seen him except one Sunday afternoon since."

"Gee, Robert, I'm really sorry," said Jennifer, "what happened?" "Well," said Robert, "for a long time it seemed like my mom and dad either were not talking to each other at all or they were arguing, yelling, and screaming at each other. They would sometimes wake me during the night. Things got worse as time went by and sometimes my dad would leave. But before he would always come back."

"My mom talked to me last night and said that dad would not be coming back this time and that they had decided to get a divorce," Robert went on. "Mom said that she and dad will have to go to court for a hearing before a judge to decide some stuff about the house, the cars, and other property they own. They will also have to decide if I'm going to live with her or with dad. She said that my little sister will stay with her, for sure, but I can talk with them about who I will live with."

"I'm really sorry to hear that, Robert," said Jennifer. "What do you think you'll do?" "I don't really know," said Robert. "I'm really confused. I'm really mad at my dad for leaving, but I miss having him at home. I sure don't want mom and dad to fight any more, but they don't seem very happy right now, anyway."

"Mom says that dad will have to pay her some money to live on, but she will have to get a job too. That means I won't be able to see her very much. I feel that it's somehow my fault that dad moved out and that they are getting a divorce."

"It's not your fault, at all," said Jennifer. "My friend Amy's parents got a divorce last year and she felt the same way. It wasn't her fault and it's not your fault, either."

"Maybe not," said Robert, "but I'm still confused and upset."

The Law

In one state, married persons may obtain a divorce only for the following reasons:

(A) Either party had another husband or wife;
(B) Willful (intended) absence of one spouse for one year or more;
(C) Extreme cruelty;
(D) Adultery;
(E) Fraudulent contract;
(F) Any gross neglect of duty;
(G) Habitual drunkenness;
(H) Imprisonment of one spouse in a state or federal penal institution;
(I) One spouse gets a divorce outside the state; as a result, the party who obtained the divorce is released from the obligations of the marriage;
(J) When husband and wife have, without interruption for two years, lived separate and apart without cohabitation.

It is also possible in some states for married persons to dissolve (or agree to end) their marriage. This action is called a dissolution of marriage. To be able to dissolve their marriage, a couple must sign, and submit to a court for approval, a written separation agreement which divides all property between them, sets forth child support and alimony, if any, to be paid, and establishes custody and visitation rights with children.

In a divorce or dissolution, custody of children is awarded to one parent or the other. The parent having custody of a child is the parent with whom the child lives and who has control of the child. Most states have statutes which state the factors to be considered in awarding custody of children, including the wishes of the child, if he or she is old enough. This is one such statute:

> Upon hearing the testimony of either or both parents . . . the court shall decide which of them shall have the care, custody, and control of the children, taking into account that which would be for their best interest, except that any child twelve years of age or more may be allowed to choose the parent with whom the child is to live unless the court finds that the parent so selected is unfitted to take charge or unless the court finds, with respect to a child twelve years of age or older, that it would not be in the best interests of the child to have the choice. Prior to trial, the court may cause an investigation to be made as to the character, family relations, past conduct, earning ability, and financial worth of the parties to the action and may order the parties and their minor children to submit to medical, psychological, and psychiatric examination.

Discussion Questions

1. Do you think that Robert should live with his mom or his dad? Why?
2. What factors are important when a court decides which parent will have custody of children?
3. For what reasons can people get a divorce in your state?
4. What is child support? Alimony? What purposes do they serve?
5. Do you know of any ways these kinds of problems can be solved?
6. Do you think Robert's father owes Robert's mother anything?
7. What responsibilities does Robert's father have to Robert and his sister?
8. What do you think about Robert's feelings that his parents' problems are his fault?

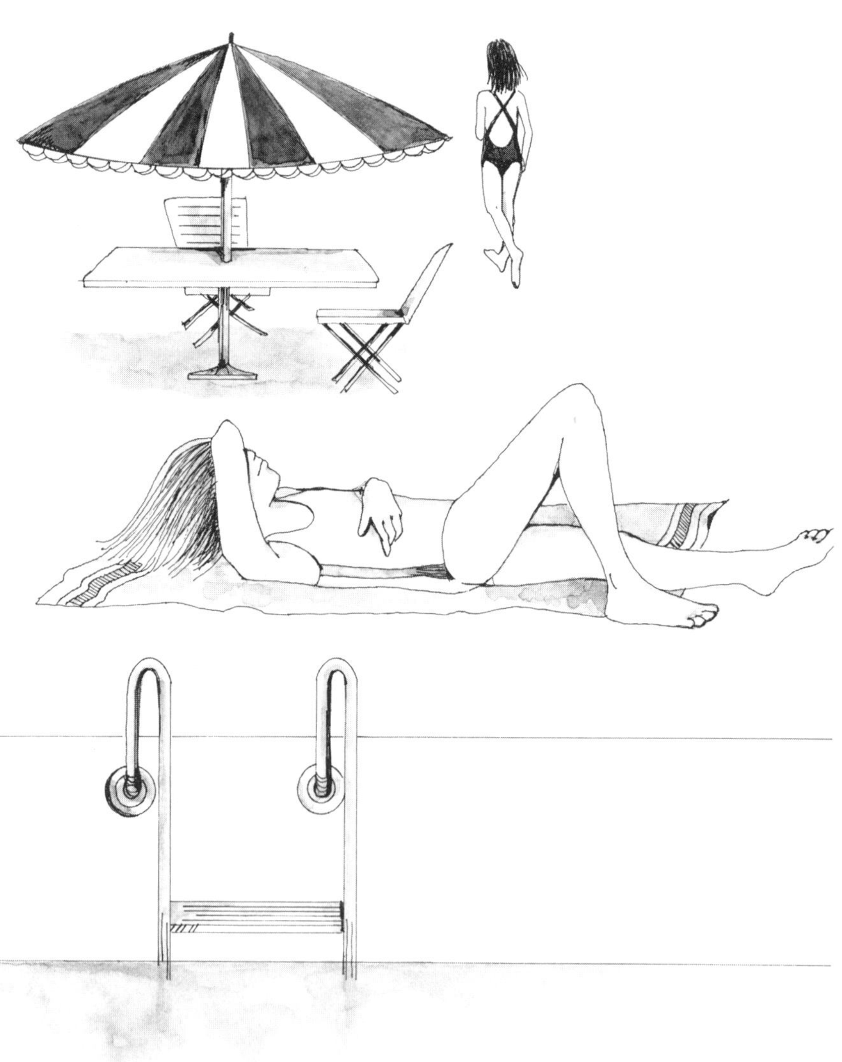

7 *Near-Tragedy at the Pool*

Jane didn't let the telephone ring a second time. She never did, if she could help it.

"Thompson residence, Jane speaking," she spoke into the mouthpiece.

"Jane, it's Mary Ann," came through the receiver. "Can you come over for a swim? They've just finished filling our pool."

"Golly, yeah, I'll be right there," Jane replied. She was delighted with the invitation, as it was about the hottest day they had had so far during vacation. Besides, she'd done her chores of cleaning her room and doing the breakfast dishes for her mother, both of her library books were finished, and there was nothing she liked on TV. It was certainly too hot to do anything out in the yard! A swim sounded just perfect on a hot day like this.

And she of course felt a whole lot warmer at the end of her three-block bicycle ride to Mary Ann's house. So they lost no time in changing into their swimming suits, and into the pool they went. The water was refreshing, almost too cold, because it had just been put into the pool and had not yet had time to warm up. The girls had to keep active, diving and jumping in, playing catch with a beach-ball, racing each other from one end to the other.

After twenty minutes or so they climbed out, chilled and shivering, to warm up in the sun for a while. Mary Ann went into the house to get some pop and chips for them to snack on. Jane put on sun-tan lotion, spread out a towel, and lay down on her back, shielding her eyes with her right arm.

She was just beginning to feel warm again when suddenly there was a high-pitched scream and a splash at the far end of the pool. Jane sat up just in time to see a small head and two thrashing arms going under. She ran about two-thirds of the way down the pool, dived in, grabbed a small arm, and came up to the edge of the pool with a small boy.

It was the neighbor's little boy, three-year-old Jason Brown. He was terribly frightened, coughing and crying, scarcely able to catch his breath. Jane sat him on the edge of the pool, climbed out, and hugged him.

"You're all right now, Jason," she told him, "you're going to be all right, I'll take you to your Mommy."

Mary Ann was coming out with the pop at the same time that Mrs. Brown came running out her back door in response to Jason's scream. She crossed through the flowerbeds, which separated the two back yards, and grabbed Jason away from Jane.

Jason was still choking and crying. Mrs. Brown was hysterical, scarcely able to speak. She turned first on Jane, "This is your fault, Jane Thompson. You were the one out here by the pool. You should have been watching. Why did you let him near the edge? Didn't you see him? Didn't you hear him? You'll pay for this!"

Then, noticing Mary Ann, who had by then come up to the others, Mrs. Brown turned on her. "It's really your fault! It's your pool! You could have killed my baby! It's your responsibility. The neighbors should never have let you put in that pool."

Mrs. Brown was, by this time, calmer, but remained angry. "I'm going to do something about this. Come on, Jason, let's go home. Mary Ann Russel, I'm going to speak to your parents about this pool. There ought to be a locked fence around it. You're all responsible. There ought to be a law. Come on, Jason, let's go home."

The two girls looked at each other.

"Well, there goes the end of a perfect day," said Jane.

"What happens next?" she asked.

"We're in hot water now," said Mary Ann.

The Law

Because there have been so many accidental deaths from children and adults falling into unattended swimming pools, most cities have passed ordinances to try to prevent situations like Jane's. One such ordinance reads as follows:

> Every outdoor swimming pool shall be completely surrounded by an approved fence . . . not less than three and one-half feet in height for family swim-

ming pools, which shall be constructed so that horizontal members are on the pool side of the enclosure and vertical members shall not be spaced more than two inches apart . . . All gates or doors opening through such enclosures shall be designed to permit locking and shall be kept locked when the pool is not in actual use, or is left unattended. . . . No person in possession of land within the City, either as owner, purchaser, lessee, tenant or a licensee, upon which is situated a swimming pool, shall fail to provide and maintain such fence or wall as herein provided. Where a swimming pool is located above ground, when the sides of the pool are forty-two inches or higher, provided all ladders are removed when not in use, they may serve as an enclosure under the terms of this section.

Discussion Questions

1. Was Mrs. Brown in any way at fault for what happened to Jason? Does she have some duty to watch Jason because he is so little?
2. Do you think ordinances like the one above help prevent accidents like Jason's?
3. Was Mary Ann's family obligated to do anything to try to prevent something like this from happening?
4. What would you have told Mrs. Brown if you had been in Mary Ann's place? In Jane's place?
5. What is the best thing to do when someone is as excited and upset as Mrs. Brown was?
6. Find out how many pools are in your city or community and if there are ordinances similar to the one above. See if you can determine why the ordinance was passed if there is one. See if you can locate the number of swimming pool accidents which have taken the lives of children who have fallen into a pool. Does this justify having everyone with a pool build a fence around it? Why? Or why not?

8 *The Oral Agreement*

With school over for the year, John had the ambition to find a summer job from which he could make enough money to buy the new knobby-wheeled motorcross bicycle he had seen in a catalog. Like many of the boys in his neighborhood, John hoped to find several people whose lawns he could mow in order to make the money he needed.

The very first house he tried was old Mr. Krochit's. Mr. Krochit was known by the neighbors as being not too friendly, but he owned a very large house with a very big lawn, a lot of trees and bushes, and a very large fence around it, all of which would require a lot of trimming. When Mr. Krochit came to the door John said, "Hi, Mr. Krochit. I'm looking for jobs cutting grass and trimming. Can you use me this summer?"

After a pause Mr. Krochit said, "John, I think I can use your services. It's getting so that lawn of mine is too big for me to cut, anymore; besides, I'm going to be away for part of the summer."

Much to John's surprise, Mr. Krochit said, "I'll pay you \$20.00 a week to cut my grass and trim along the fence and around the trees and bushes. This is a big job, and if I'm going to pay you that much, I want you to do a good job, so I don't think you should work for anyone else in the neighborhood."

John agreed, since he could see that it would take him most of each week to do all that would have to be done, leaving a couple of days clear for swimming and Little League and taking care of his own yard. The \$20.00 a week would give him more than enough to buy his bicycle and some spending money for his vacation. Mr. Krochit said, "John, I'm going on a trip Saturday, so you can begin next week."

John was thrilled with his new job and immediately ran home and told his father. "It'll be great, Dad, but I'll have to buy a sickle and clippers. Mr. Krochit won't let me use his tools, so I'll have to use our mower, too."

"I think I can help you there, John," said his father. "Sure, you can use our mower, and I'll lend you the money for the other tools." So John borrowed the money from his father and bought the sickle and clippers which he needed to do all the trimming around Mr. Krochit's lawn. Those tools cost him $27.00. "I'll replay you in no time, Dad, and still have plenty for my bike," John promised.

As he had been told to do, John returned to Mr. Krochit's house the next week and immediately began work on Mr. Krochit's lawn. He worked hard for three days straight, mowing Mr. Krochit's grass, trimming the hedges and clipping the grass around the fence. "It's really hard work," John would tell his Mother each evening, "but it will be worth it."

At the end of those three long days John was getting ready to head for home when who should come out the front door but Mr. Krochit. John said, "I thought you had gone away for the week. I just completed the first week's work and you can pay me now, if it's O.K." "No, I don't intend to pay you for the poor job you've done, and, what's more, I don't want you to come back any more this summer!"

John was very angry and upset that he was not to be paid for the work which he had done. He was in debt to his father for special tools which he had bought, and he would probably have no more work that summer. Because John thought that he would be working all summer for Mr. Krochit, he had not asked anyone else if he could do their yard work. By this time the other boys in the neighborhood had taken all of the other jobs.

"I think Mr. Krochit just didn't want to pay me for the weeks he was going to be gone this summer," John said to his dad later.

As a result John was unable to repay his father for the tools which he had bought, and he was unable to buy the special bike he had wanted so much for so long.

The Law

The Common Law of most states deals with situations like John's. The agreement between John and Mr. Krochit is called a contract. It may be in writing; or it may be an oral contract—that is, a spoken agreement—like John's. A contract is really a set of promises between persons that one will do one thing if the other will do something else.

When one person doesn't do what he promised the other person, it is said that he has breached the agreement. And when a person breaches an agreement, he usually owes the other person what the person would have received if the other had not breached the agreement.

Discussion Questions

1. What do you call the agreement between John and Mr. Krochit?
2. What were the promises which Mr. Krochit and John made to each other?
3. Do you think that what Mr. Krochit did to John was fair? Why? Why not?
4. Who "breached" their agreement?
5. Do you think that Mr. Krochit should be allowed to break his promise?
6. Does John owe anything to Mr. Krochit? Does Mr. Krochit owe John anything?
7. Have you heard of small claims court? Look into this provision and decide whether you think the judge would award John his payment.
8. If in fact, John's work was not fully satisfactory—if the trimming was not neat, if some bushes or flowers had been damaged—how should the matter be settled?

9 *The Pellet Gun*

It was mid-afternoon on a Saturday, time for Billy to bike over to the newspaper drop to pick up the newspapers for his paper route. He had been playing with his friend Jack, who decided to ride along with him.

As they neared the corner where the papers were dropped, Billy pointed to a house which they were approaching and told Jack, "That's where the Moustafis live. They moved here just a couple of months ago. Mr. and Mrs. Moustafis can hardly speak any English at all. There's a family here in town who sponsors them. They have a son about our age named Ata. He speaks some English, but I haven't had much chance to get to know him at school; he's in the bilingual program or special education or something. That's him out in the side yard."

"Hey, look," said Jack, "he's target-practicing with a B-B gun or pellet gun, maybe a .22, even."

"I think it must be a pellet gun," said Billy, "that's maybe not quite as powerful as a .22, but it's a lot more powerful than a B-B gun, you know."

As the boys came in front of Ata's house, they waved and Billy called out, "Hi, Ata, great-looking pellet gun."

Ata looked up, but he didn't say anything, as if not understanding. He didn't wave back for several seconds. Then, just as the boys had turned back and were proceeding down the street, Ata turned toward them, and appeared to be aiming the gun in their direction as the pellet gun went off.

Jack, who was riding a little bit ahead, heard Billy yell, "Ouch, my arm!"

Jack looked back to see Billy grab at his right arm with his left hand, lose control of his bike, and fall to the street.

Jack braked his bike, turned around, and came back to where Billy and his bike lay. "My gosh, you've been shot!" he exclaimed, examining the small dark-bluish hole oozing blood in Billy's forearm.

"Boy, it sure hurts," Billy moaned. He had also skinned his left arm and knee and bumped his head on the pavement.

Jack got Billy and his bike out of the street, left him resting on the sidewalk, and went to a nearby house and phoned Billy's parents. They arrived in only a few minutes and rushed Billy to the emergency room at the hospital.

At the hospital a doctor talked afterward with Billy's mother and father about what had been done for Billy.

"Billy was very lucky," said the doctor, "it could have been an eye. No veins or arteries or tendons were damaged, and the wound was only an inch or so deep. His bumps and scrapes are not serious, though that bump on his forehead could have been; bikers should always wear helmets. We had to perform minor surgery to remove that pellet from Billy's arm. Again, it's not serious, and he can go home with you as soon as the incision is bandaged. We'll want to see him again in a couple of days, though, to check him over and remove the stitches.

The doctor then changed the subject: "We'll need some further information from you and Billy about what happened. Whenever we treat a gunshot wound like this, we have to report it to the police for them to investigate." When Billy joined them, he told the doctor all he could remember, and the doctor put it down in his report, adding his own accounts of the nature of the wound and the medical treatment. Jack said, "Ata might have been waving the gun at us after we waved at him, but it sure looked like he was aiming at us." "One thing more," the doctor added, "you can probably expect the police to call to see you about this, too."

And that evening a police officer did come to their house to talk with them about what had happened. He too made out a report and assured them that the police would look further into the matter.

"You may know," the policeman said, "since this Ata Moustafis is pretty clearly responsible, then his parents should pay for the hospital bills and pay to have Billy's bike repaired. This state has a law which requires that they pay for what their son did. There could also be other charges, but that part of it is up to you."

The next evening the Moustafis' sponsors, Mr. and Mrs. Jones, called Billy's parents; they had, some years before, served in the Peace Corps in the Moustafis' native land,

and so they knew their language. They had assisted the police in talking with Ata's parents, serving as interpreters.

The investigation established that the shooting was clearly an accident. Both Ata and his parents were very sorry for what occurred. All the bills were paid and Billy's arm was soon all right. Billy's parents did not press any other charges.

The Law

In one state, a statute has been passed to deal with situations like this one. It is as follows:

> Any person is entitled to maintain an action to recover compensatory damages in a civil action, in an amount not to exceed two thousand dollars and costs of suit in a court of competent jurisdiction, from the parents having the custody and control of a minor under the age of eighteen years, who willfully and maliciously assaults such person by a means or force likely to produce great bodily harm.

Discussion Questions

1. What do you think should happen to Ata?
2. If you were Ata's parents, what would you do to Ata?
3. Does your state have a law that requires parents to pay for damages resulting from their child's conduct? If so, do you think it is a good law? If not, do you think your state should have one?
4. What could have been done to prevent this incident?
5. Should people be allowed to possess firearms, even B-B or pellet guns? At what minimum age? What restrictions should be placed on their use? Should their use be allowed within city limits?
6. What further (criminal) charge(s) should be brought against Ata? Against his parents?

10 *The Accident*

One afternoon Jane and her mother were driving in their car on the way to the grocery store, as they needed to pick up a few things for dinner before going home. Jane's mother worked as a secretary and had picked Jane up after school. "How was school today, Jane?" her mother asked. "School was fine, Mom," answered Jane, "look at the good grades I got on my papers today." "Not now, dear, not while I'm driving," Jane's mother replied; she was a very careful driver and always watched out for other cars and also watched all around the car.

As they were approaching an intersection, Jane said, "Mother, we're in luck; the traffic light is green." "That's good," said Jane's mother "but you have to look for traffic anyway." She checked for other cars and proceeded to go through the intersection.

Just as the car reached the middle of the intersection, a car that was traveling very fast came down the intersecting street, and drove on into the intersection; the driver had ignored the red light. The other car struck their car on the driver's side. Jane and her mother were thrown around inside the car and both were injured very badly. The attending policeman later said that they were saved from being killed because they both had their seat belts buckled, which kept them from being thrown from the car.

The driver of the other car got out of his car and could hardly stand up. Some people at the accident thought that he was hurt. "Hey, mister, are you O.K.? Did you hit your head?" asked a man who saw the accident. "But that was pretty dumb, speeding through that red light!" "Leave me alone," growled the other driver to the man. "I didn't hurt myself, and I didn't see any red light."

"Boy, do you smell that guy's breath!" said the man on the sidewalk to a lady nearby. "He's been drinking a lot. I'm surprised he was able to drive his car at all." "The other car didn't even have a chance to avoid his hitting it," said the lady.

They later learned that the other driver was not hurt badly. The police tested the man's blood to see if it contained alcohol and found that it did. In fact, there was so much alcohol in the man's blood that he was considered "legally drunk" according to the Statutory Law of Jane's state. It came out in the investigation that the man had been drinking at a bar for several hours before the accident.

Jane and her mother were taken to the hospital in an ambulance. Jane's mother had many broken bones and serious internal injuries. Jane's head had been hit very hard and her hips were broken. They each remained in the hospital for a month before they were then able to leave.

The bill at the hospital was very large because of all the necessary surgery and because of the length of Jane's and her mother's stay. The other driver's car insurance paid for some, but not all, of these costs, since he was underinsured for so serious an accident. Jane's mother was never able to walk after the accident and was confined to a wheelchair; she was in and out of the hospital many times and was unable to work any longer. Jane was left with a stiff-legged limp. Also, Jane's father had to buy a new car—entirely with his own money—because their car had been completely wrecked.

The Law

Accidents like Jane's and her mother's are often the result of one persons's "negligence." Negligence is a concept developed through the Common Law and is often defined as follows:

> Negligence is frequently defined as the want (lack) of ordinary care, or failure to exercise ordinary care. Negligence is the failure to do what a reasonable and prudent man would ordinarly have done under the circumstances of the situation, or not doing what such a person, under the existing circumstances, would not have done.

Statutes or ordinances often establish what constitutes ordinary care in the particular situation. If a person violates the statute, he is negligent.

Accidents are too often caused by persons who are driving while intoxicated. Statutes have been enacted in each state prohibiting that act. Many are similar to this one:

No person who is under the influence of alcohol or any drug of abuse shall operate any vehicle within this state.

These statutes must also define when a person is "under the influence of alcohol." That determination is usually made based upon the amount of alcohol found in a person's blood. If the alcohol content is a certain amount, a person is presumed—that is, automatically considered to be—under the influence of alcohol. One such definition is as follows:

In any criminal prosecution for a violation of this statute or the ordinance of any municipality relating to driving a vehicle while under the influence of alcohol, the court may admit evidence on the concentration of alcohol in the defendant's blood at the time of the alleged violation as shown by chemical analysis of the defendant's blood, urine, breath, or other bodily substance withdrawn within two hours of the time of such alleged violation.

If there was at that time a concentration of less than ten hundredths of one per cent (.10%) by weight of alcohol, but more than five hundredths of one per cent (.05%) by weight of alcohol, in the defendant's blood, such fact shall not give rise to any presumption that the defendant was or was not under the influence of alcohol, but such fact may be considered with other competent evidence in determining the guilt or innocence of the defendant.

If there was at that time a concentration of ten hundredths of one per cent (.10%) or more by weight of alcohol in the defendant's blood, it shall be presumed that the defendant was under the influence of alcohol.

If there was at the time a concentration of five hundredths of one per cent (.05%) or less by weight of alcohol in the defendant's blood, it shall be presumed that the defendant was not under the influence of alcohol.

Discussion Questions

1. Have you ever known anyone who was in an auto accident? What happened to that person?
2. What did the other driver do that was wrong? Why was it wrong?

3. Does the driver of the other car owe anything to Jane or her mother and father?
4. Do you know what insurance is? How does insurance work? What kind of insurance does your mother and father have? Can insurance ever make up for someone who, after an accident, must spend the rest of his or her life in a wheelchair?
5. What do you think could be done to prevent accidents like this? How was the other driver negligent?
6. What do you think should be done with people who drink and drive? Does the law in your state say anything special about people who drink and drive?

11 *One Thing Leads to Another*

It was a Saturday morning, getting close to noon-time. Jeff and Tommy, middle school students, came down the street on their bicycles, slowing and signalling as they turned into Jeff's driveway.

Several houses away, Tim and Steve, high school Juniors, were playing one-on-one basketball in Tim's driveway. Jeff admired his neighbor Tim very much, especially for his ability in basketball. Tim had been a promising player in the middle school, and he went on to make the varsity team in high school, but then he was dropped from the team by the coach. Tim never talked about why he had been dropped, but people who knew him figured quite correctly that it was because he wouldn't follow the training rules; he smoked cigarettes, drank beer, drove around town until late at night, neglected his studies, and he just wasn't a team player—Tim always did just as he pleased.

Jeff and Tommy waved to Tim and Steve as they turned in. Tim waved back, gestering for them to come over. The younger boys jumped at the chance to play with the ''big guys,'' as Tommy put it, adding, ''Boy, this is going to be fun!''

After they had been playing Tim and Jeff against Steve and Tommy for about half an hour, Tim invited them inside: ''Let's go play ping-pong in the rec room, and I'll fix us some snacks and drinks. I'll bet you're as hungry as I am.''

''Okay, ping pong is my game,'' said Steve. ''I'll bet I can beat all of you.''

''Come again, big guy,'' Jeff answered, ''I'll take you on.''

As soon as they entered the recreation room, Jeff and Steve grabbed paddles and were soon into a game. Tim went into the kitchen to get some snacks, and Tommy watched the ping-pong game, cheering his friend Jeff and then Steve as they made good shots. Jeff was actually getting the better of Steve, staying ahead throughout the game, which ended 21-19.

Steve remarked admiringly, "By golly, Jeff you're pretty good at this, I have to admit it. But I'm just getting warmed up, so next time you'd better be prepared for the licking of your life." This kind of talk made Jeff and Tommy feel really great, these two high school boys inviting them to join in their activities and treating them as equals.

Tim came back to the rec room from the kitchen with a great collection of snacks, mostly "junk food" — potato chips, pretzels, corn curls, and the like. He also had a six-pack of beer.

"Come on, guys, eat up," Tim invited them. My folks won't be home til late tonight, so we'll also help ourselves to the beer."

Tim and Steve immediately opened cans of beer and started drinking them, but Jeff and Tommy hung back, only taking some of the snacks.

"Tim, could I please have some pop or a glass of water instead," Jeff asked, "I'm really thirsty."

"Come on, Jeff," said Tim, "you and Tommy have a beer with us."

"No, I can't drink beer. I'm not old enough, and I've never had more than a little taste before. What's more," Jeff added, "my dad would bust me one if he caught me."

Tommy felt pretty much the same way as Jeff, saying, "I think maybe I'd better be getting home. My mom will be expecting me for lunch."

But Tim cut them both off. "What kind of kids are you, anyway, a couple babies? I thought you were regular guys. If this is the way you are we won't ask you to play basketball again with us. Come on have a beer; you'll like it-make a man of you, get you ready for high school."

Well, Jeff thought, it was real neat to be there with these two high school guys, so he took a big drink of the beer which was opened for him, and Tommy decided to do the same thing. "Just you guys keep it quiet about this," Jeff asked, "so I don't get into a lot of trouble at home—or at school." "That's a deal," Tim said.

So Jeff and Tommy each finished their beers, Tim and Steve having two apiece. When they went back to the ping-pong game, the playing was very sloppy as they drank more beer and all four of them were loud and acting very silly, hitting the balls all over the room.

Tim suddenly interrupted everything with, "Hey, guys, we've got to go get some more beer before my parents get home to replace what we drank. My mother's car is here and I know a drive-in where they sell it without asking for proof of your age."

Jeff and Tommy were excited about going along on this adventure, so they got into the car too. Tim took off with the tires loudly "burning rubber" for half a block or so.

"I feel a little dizzy," Tommy complained.

"Just open your window and stick your head out in the fresh air," Steve advised, "then you'll feel better."

"Hey, Tim, please don't drive so fast. I'm getting sick to my stomach too," Jeff said.

"Oh, come on you guys," Tim half-turned to tell them in the back seat, "I'm a good driver. Even my dad tells me I am."

Tim had just gotten the words out of his mouth when he went through a stop sign, only narrowly missing a car on the through street.

"Hey, buddy, slow this thing down," Steve yelled. But Tim just kept pushing on the accelerator, going faster and faster.

They had just left the drive-in with their purchase of two six-packs of beer when Tim saw in the rear-view mirror the red flashing lights a block or so behind him. His answer to that was to step on the gas and turn a corner, then another.

Steve said to Tim, "you'd better park this thing and let us all out," but Tim just drove faster and more wildly, answering, "Do you know what they'll do to us if they catch us?"

Jeff was nearly crying by this time, "I want to go home. Let me out."

"Shut up, you baby," Tim snapped back. "I can't afford to get caught. The police must have seen us coming out of the drive-in, or maybe somebody reported us about that stop sign or speeding."

As they turned yet another corner, with the tires squealing, Tim found himself on a dead end street. As he turned again, there was a car backing out of a driveway. Tim swerved to miss that car, but he slammed into one of a row of parked cars, and his car overturned and came to rest against the porch of one of the houses. Smoke poured from the car as the police car pulled up and a crowd began to gather.

The Law

Driving a vehicle while drinking or while under the influence of alcohol is a very serious matter because of the increased nature of someone being hurt or of damage to the property of others. Most states have strong penalties for such an offense as a result.

In one state, the offense is punished by imprisonment for up to six months and a fine of up to One thousand dollars ($1,000). A judge must give the person a minimum punishment of three days imprisonment and a one hundred fifty dollar fine. The minimum punishment is worse for people who commit the offense more than once.

Additionally, a person's driver's license must be suspended so he cannot drive at all for at least 30 days and the person may have to purchase very expensive insurance before he can drive again.

When the person driving under the influence of alcohol is a minor and he injures someone or causes damage to property, the law requires his parents to pay all costs of the other person's injury and to pay for the damage to the other person's property.

Finally, when either an adult or a minor gives a minor alcohol, whether they want it or not, he may be guilty of contributing to the delinquency of a minor, and may be punished separately for that offense. This particularly is the case when the minor causes some damage to another person as a result of having drunk the alcohol.

Discussion Questions

1. What happens next?
2. What kind of ending do you see for this story?
3. Consider the costs in this case—a car (or two cars) totally wrecked, perhaps a house set afire, probably some bodily injuries, crippling, etc.; one or more of the boys might be killed.
4. When did things go wrong? At what point could Jeff and Tommy still have avoided trouble?

5. Are the laws about drinking adequate to save lives? How might they be enforced more effectively?
6. What are the potential hazards of middle school boys or girls seeking association and approval of older youth? Can you think of how older youth can help younger boys and girls to grow up safely?
7. Do you see some lessons in this story that might help parents with their children?
8. How can your school program help you to face these kinds of problems.

12 *Keith's Best Friend*

Rickie came to school one day with bruises all over his face and arms. "My gosh, Rickie," his friend Keith observed, "you look like you've lost an awful fight." Rickie wouldn't tell him what had happened, but Keith wouldn't give up, since Rickie was his best school friend. He said, "Rickie, you just tell me who did it, and I'll take care of him." Keith being a big boy for his age and Rickie being somewhat small and not very strong, Keith had always taken his part with other kids.

When they were alone on the playground at lunch time, Keith again asked Rickie what had happened to him, "Rickie, I'm your best friend; I'm not going to let anyone beat on you." With tears in his eyes Rickie said, "Keith, my dad comes home drunk and shouts at my mom and picks on me. Last night I stood in front of my mom when he was pushing her around and he grabbed me and hit me and shoved me around the room." As Rickie continued to cry he said, "He hurt me so much I hardly slept all night because I was afraid he would come into the room and do it some more. I heard him hollering at my mom all night." Keith said, "Gee, Rickie, I don't know what I can do to help, but I'll sure try." Then Keith thought to himself, "I'll ask my mom if Rickie can come stay at our house."

As soon as Keith got home from school he opened the front door and called to his mother. She came to the hall where Keith was waiting and said, "What's wrong? Why are you so upset?" Keith said, "It's Rickie. He's got a real big problem and I really don't know what to do about it." His mother put her arm around Keith and they went to the living room and sat on the sofa together.

Keith said, "Mother, Rickie's dad has been beating up on him and today he came to school all bruised up. Mother, couldn't Rickie come and stay with us; I'll share my room with him—please." "Keith," said his mother, "we would be glad to have Rickie to stay with us for a while, but that wouldn't solve the problem. I'll talk it over with your dad when he comes home and we will see what we can do that would be best for Rickie." "Thanks mom," said Keith.

Later that night Keith was called by his mother to come talk with her and his dad. "Keith, we have at least two possible ways of solving Rickie's problem," said Keith's mother. "I could talk with the principal or the school counselor about Rickie and let one of them contact the proper authorities. Or I could call the Child Abuse Center myself and report to them. I won't even have to give them my name." Keith's dad said, "I think there is a law that would protect Rickie from abuse by his father." Keith was happy that something could be done to help his friend. Both of Keith's parents assured him that they would take some action.

The Law

Most states have statutes designed to help in situations like Rickie's. Such statutes are designed to protect, among others, abused or neglected children. An "abused child" includes any child whose life, health, or safety is endangered by another, or who exhibits evidence of any injury or death caused other than by accidental means.

A "dependent child" is defined as any child who is homeless or destitute or without proper care or support, through no fault of his parents, guardian, or custodian or whose condition or environment is such as to require the state, in the interests of the child, to assume his guardianship.

In the case of a neglected or abused child, state law often provides the procedure to be followed to protect the child. In one state, the procedure is established by statute, as follows:

> Any person having knowledge of a child who appears to be . . . abused, neglected, or dependent may, with respect to such child, file a sworn complaint in the juvenile court . . . in settlement. Such sworn complaint may be upon information and belief, and in addition to the allegation that the child is . . . abused, neglected, or dependent . . . the complaint must allege the particular facts upon which the allegation of abuse, neglect (or) dependency is based.

> If, based upon a hearing and the complaint, it is determined that a child is abused or neglected, the state juvenile authorities will take custody of the child to protect it or to meet its needs.

Discussion Questions

1. What would you do if a friend told you about getting frequent beatings which left bruises all over his/her body?
2. Is there a law that protects children in your town or state? Do you think there should be such a law?
3. Should parents who have problems like this see a minister or marriage counselor?
4. Would it have been the right thing for Keith's family to do to take Rick into their home?
5. Should other people, such as Keith's family, get involved in the problems of other families, such as the one Rick had?

13 *Don't Let It Happen To You*

Betsy was putting her lunch in her locker when she noted Jeannie slipping a small bag to Sue in exchange for some money. Betsy couldn't see how much money it was, but she did see the green of a bill. Just before lunch Betsy went to her locker to get her lunch and again she met Jeannie there. Jeannie was opening her locker when Roger came by and Jeannie said, "I've got some for you today, Roger." Roger then handed Jeannie something, which was not clearly seen by Betsy, and Jeannie passed him a small bag. As Roger left, Betsy said, "Jeannie, is your class selling something to raise money; I'll buy something to help you." With that Jeannie said, "Stay out of this; this is my business." Then she walked away from Betsy.

Betsy took her lunch and went to the lunch room to eat, but she was bothered by Jeannie's answer to her. That afternoon Sue acted very strange in class. She kept her head down on her desk and when called on to answer a question by Ms. Frame she answered louder than usual that she didn't know the answer. The class laughed at the way she answered. Ms. Frame asked, "Sue, are you not feeling well?" Sue replied, "I'm just great." Again the class broke out into a loud laugh. Ms. Frame continued her discussion with the class, but she also kept an eye on Sue from time to time.

When class was over, Sue was slow to leave the room and Betsy walked out with her. She asked Sue if she could walk home with her and Sue replied in a loud, slurred voice, "Why, I feel just great." As the girls were walking toward their homes, Sue became dizzy and was unable to walk straight. She also appeared to be having some trouble breathing. Betsy put her arm around her and helped her to the door of her house. Mrs. Robins came to the door. She said, "Sue, are you sick again?" But Sue didn't answer. Betsy said, "I'm afraid she's catching something; she got weaker as we got closer to home." Mrs. Robins thanked Betsy for helping to bring Sue home and Betsy walked the half block to her home. Along the way she couldn't stop thinking about what she had seen at the school locker.

The next day at school Betsy saw several other kids buying something from Jeannie on the playground. During the morning she also noticed that Sue was in school. When she had the opportunity she said, "Sue, how are you making it today?" Sue replied, "Not so good, but I'll do better if you lend me a dollar until tomorrow." Betsy said, "If it will help and if you'll give it back to me tomorrow, I'll be glad to." Betsy took the dollar from her shoulder bag and gave it to Sue. At lunch time, as she was going to her locker, she noticed Sue running to Jeannie's locker about the same time that Jeannie got there. As Betsy reached her locker and started to open it, she heard Jeannie say, "Sue, you need another dollar." Sue said, "Please, Jeannie, I'll get it tomorrow." Jeannie said, "You'd better, or else!" "I will! I will!" replied Sue, and Jeannie put a small bag in her hand. Betsy was now becoming very curious about what was happening to Sue.

Sue seemed to disappear during the lunch hour and when her name was called for science class she wasn't present. Betsy was very disturbed over this and told the teacher after class that Sue had gone home sick after school yesterday, but that she said she felt O.K. this morning. The teacher, Mr. Schultz, said, "I'll look into it."

As soon as school was out Betsy went to look for Jeannie and found her on the corner of the school parking lot. She was surrounded by a number of other girls and boys. Betsy was hesitant but she called out to Jeannie and said, "Jeannie have you seen Sue since lunch?" Jeannie shouted back, "Forget it, Goodie-Goodie, it's none of your business where she is." With that the other kids laughed at Betsy and Betsy headed for home.

Mrs. Robins saw Betsy coming down the street and she looked to see if Sue was following her. She asked Betsy, "Have you seen Sue since school was out?" Betsy replied, "No, I haven't, Mrs. Robins, but if I see her I'll tell her you're looking for her." Mrs. Robins said, "Betsy I've been worried about her grades lately, as she comes home sick every day and she doesn't get her homework done." Betsy paused, then said, "I asked her how she was this morning and she said she was feeling great." Betsy was reluctant to say anything to Mrs. Robins about what she had seen taking place between Jeannie and Sue.

When Betsy got home she found a note from her mother saying that she would be home a little late today, as she had to finish up some work at the office. The note asked Betsy to start supper. Betsy went to her room to start her homework, but she couldn't concentrate on it, thinking about what was going on in school; and she was worried about what happened to Sue, since she hadn't seen her at school that afternoon.

As Betsy was heading for the kitchen to start fixing supper the phone rang. Betsy picked up the phone and said, "Hello!" In a low voice, which made it almost impossible to understand what was being said, someone said, "Betsy, help me . . . help me." Betsy shouted into the phone. "Sue, is that you?" No reply came back as Betsy kept saying, "Sue! Sue! Where are you? Tell me where you are." After a long pause she heard the words "Tennis courts . . . park." At that moment Betsy's mother, Mrs. Honaker, came in and heard Betsy say, "Sue, stay where you are; we'll come get you; stay where you are."

Mrs. Honaker asked, "Betsy, what's this all about?" Betsy said, "Please, mother, leave a note for daddy telling him we'll be right back. Please take me to Mrs. Robins' house, then we'll go get Sue and I'll tell you on the way what happened." Mrs. Honaker wrote a quick note on the message board by the phone for Mr. Honaker. Betsy phoned Mrs. Robins, whom she found beside herself with worry over not hearing from Sue. She had called the principal, but he said Mr. Schultz told him that Sue must have gone home sick at lunch time, since she was not in school that afternoon. The principal said that Ms. Frame had also talked to him. Betsy said, "Mrs. Robins, don't worry; we're coming for you and I know where Sue is. We'll go get her."

After picking up Mrs. Robins, Betsy told her and her mother what she had seen. Betsy said, "I was afraid to say anything about Jeannie's actions to anyone, since there always was a gang around her and she has been very mean at times and I really never did see what I suspected was some kind of drugs."

As they approached the tennis courts on the edge of the park, they didn't see Sue anywhere. They went toward the telephone booth at the edge of the park where Sue must have called from, but she was not there either. Mrs. Robins was becoming hysterical and Mrs. Honaker was trying to calm her. About that time a police car stopped and Betsy told the officer that they were looking for her friend who must have made a call from the phone near the edge of the park and the tennis courts. Betsy said, with tears in her eyes, "I told her to wait here at the phone." The policeman called in on his radio to have other police cars dispatched for a search through the park.

As Betsy and the officer walked down the path in the park, they saw Sue lying under some trees, all battered, as though she had been in a fight, and she was having difficulty breathing. The officer ran to his car and called for the first aid squad while Betsy stayed with Sue. Mrs. Robins saw the policeman running to his car and she became panic-stricken, shouting, "Did you find her, is she alive!" The policeman assured her she would be all right as he retraced his steps to the place where Betsy was caring for Sue, with both mothers hurrying behind him.

How Sue had got to the park and why she was so battered was not to be answered just now. In moments the ambulance was there and the crew was administering first aid as they carried Sue on the stretcher for her trip to the hospital. Just before being placed in the vehicle Sue opened her eyes and saw her mother. Mrs. Robins leaned over and kissed Sue and she got in the ambulance with her.

As Betsy's mother drove home Betsy was crying and saying, "If only I had told someone what I saw, all this might not have happened." Betsy's mother tried to comfort her by saying, "But you didn't see what was in the bag, did you?" "No," said Betsy, "but I knew something was going on that was not good for Sue. I could have told the principal, but I was afraid I might get into trouble with the other kids if I went to adults."

The Law

What does the law in your community say about selling drugs?

Such statutory law has been enacted having to do with the control of drugs. Because drugs, often referred to as "controlled substances", are so dangerous, any act associated with them is controlled and violations are severely punished. In addition to the crime of drug abuse, which in one state is defined as knowingly obtaining, possessing, or using a controlled substance, consider these additional drug-related offenses:

Corrupting Another With Drugs

No person shall knowingly do any of the following: (1) By force, threat, or deception, administer (give) to another or induce (persuade) or cause another to use a controlled substance;

(2) By any means, administer (give) or furnish to another or induce (persuade) or cause another to use a controlled substance with purpose to cause serious physical harm to such person, or with purpose to cause such person to become drug-dependent;

(3) By any means, administer (give) or furnish to another or induce (persuade) or cause another to use a controlled substance, and thereby cause serious physical harm to such person, or cause such person to become drug-dependent;

(4) By any means, furnish (give) or administer to a person under age eighteen who is at least four years his junior, or induce or cause a person under age eighteen who is at least four years his junior to use a controlled substance.

Trafficking (Dealing) In Drugs

No person shall knowingly (while aware of what he is doing) do any of the following:

(1) Sell or offer to sell a controlled substance . . .

(2) Prepare for distribution, or distribute a controlled substance, when the offender knows or has reasonable cause to believe such drug is intended for sale . . .;

(3) Cultivate (grow), manufacture, or otherwise (produce) . . . a controlled substance;

(4) Provide money or other items of value to another person with the purpose that the recipient . . . use them to obtain controlled substances for the purpose of selling or offering to sell such controlled substances . . .

Discussion Questions

1. Which of the above offenses were committed by Jeannie and her friends?
2. Would you tell your teacher or principal if you thought one of your classmates was selling drugs? If not, why not? Would you be willing to tell your classmates' parents? Why? Or why not?
3. Do you think it's wrong to tell on someone who is breaking the law?
4. If you were Betsy, what would you have done about Jeannie?
5. Are you afraid of what your friends would say about you if you told on someone for selling drugs or giving drugs to one of your classmates? If you are afraid, why?
6. Do you know that some drugs can destroy your body and your mind? If you do, why would you not tell on someone who was trafficking in drugs?
7. What would you have done if you had seen Jeannie collecting money and giving your classmates something in a bag?
8. Do you think the principal has the right to search your locker?
9. Should we put our parents or guardians through all the pain and misery that Mrs. Robins suffered if we feel we have enough evidence that something illegal is taking place?
10. Do you think Betsy had enough evidence to justify telling her parents, telling Mrs. Robins, or telling the principal?
11. Should you tell someone if you are threatened by a classmate?

14 *The New House*

A big two-story house was being built across the street from Russell's home. It was interesting and fun to watch the various workmen—the masons, carpenters, plumbers, electricians—as they did their special things. Russell's father frequently took him over there to explain how a house is built from stage to stage. But they honored the big KEEP OUT sign in front, doing all their inspecting from the sidewalk.

Some of the other boys in the neighborhood, however, liked the house for a different reason. When the workmen were not there, they went in and played around in it. They climbed around from the basement to the second floor to the attic. They often took lumber and nails and other materials to build things. Some of them took the wood and other building supplies just to be taking them.

One day after the carpenters and others had left, two of the older neighborhood boys, Jay and a friend, called to Russell, "Hey, come on over with us to play in the new house."

Russell replied, "No, I can't go in there. My parents won't let me. You see that 'keep out' sign, don't you? Besides, I'm going to play catch with Brian in my back yard."

"Okay, chicken, don't," Jay said.

Jay's friend added, "See you later, goody-goody!"

The two boys left laughing at Russell.

A little later, as Russell and Brian were playing catch, Brian asked Russell, "Did you hear that sound of breaking glass?"

They ran around to the front of Russell's house, immediately noticing the broken second-story window. Next a board came flying through one of the first-floor windows, spraying broken glass all over the front porch and the walk of the house. Then they heard a loud banging coming from upstairs. They looked up to see a siding board come falling down; Jay and his friends must have kicked it until it came loose.

At that very moment the contractor drove up to check on the progress of the building. He saw the damage that had been done and as Jay came running out the opening for the front door he grabbed him by one arm and held on to him. Jay's friend, seeing from inside what had happened, ducked out the back and ran home. The contractor then pulled an unwilling and complaining Jay over to his pickup truck and called the police on his Citizens Band radio.

Jay and his parents had to go to Juvenile Court. The judge told Jay that he must be punished, as a crime/misdemeanor had been committed, that the punishment could range all the way from probation to confinement in a child correctional school with a requirement to repay the injured party for the loss. Since this was Jay's first offense, the judge concluded, Jay would have to report to a special counselor each week for six months. Jay was reluctant to name the friend who had been with him, and the judge did not pressure him to do so.

Jay didn't have the money to pay for what he'd done, and his parents claimed that they couldn't afford to. So the builder had to replace the two windows and the broken boards at an additional cost of over five hundred dollars.

The Law

Some states have passed laws which apply to situations like this.

In one state the statute is as follows:

> Any owner of property may maintain a civil action in a court . . . to recover compensatory damages not exceeding three thousand dollars and costs of suit from the parents having custody of a minor under the age of eighteen years, who willfully damages property belonging to such owner or who commits acts cognizable as a "theft offense . . ."

Discussion Questions

1. Is it a good idea to play around in a house while it is being built? Why not?
2. Was Jay wrong by even going into the house in the first place?

3. Do you know anyone who, like Jay, has had to go to Juvenile Court and talk to a judge for doing something like this? If so, do you know what the judge said to the person?
4. Jay did not have the money to pay for the window and to replace the boards. Do you think that someone other than the owner or contractor should have to pay for them?
5. Do you know if your state has a law which would require Jay's parents to pay for these things?
6. Find out what is meant in law by an "attractive nuisance." What is the law with respect to the age at which a juvenile is responsible? Is it enough that a person is able to read a "keep-out" sign?
7. The "crime" here is that of trespassing plus malicious mischief; what is the law on these offenses? What penalties are there?

15 *Finder's Keepers?*

Mrs. Marks had some shopping to do after she picked up her daughter Carol and their neighbor Cathy Copes after school. On their way to the mall she told them, "Now, be back at the car by 4:30. I don't have a whole lot to buy, and I still have most of supper to get ready. That'll give you almost an hour."

The girls were out of the car as soon as Mrs. Marks had parked. They took off, half-running toward the video-games room. Mrs. Marks went on to the supermarket.

"Come on, Cathy," said Carol, we have to get there before it's crowded or we won't get to play."

As the girls were hurrying across the parking lot, Cathy saw a small piece of paper flutter to the ground away from a man who was just leaving his parked car, several rows from them.

"Wait up, Carol," called Cathy, heading in his direction, "I want to see what that paper is." As she got closer, a gust of wind blew the little piece of paper toward her, and Cathy then recognized what it was. "Hey, Carol, come over here," she added, "I'm pretty sure it's money." What Cathy soon had in her grasp was a twenty-dollar bill.

Cathy had it on the tip of her tongue to call out "Hey, Mister!" But when she looked around, the man was nowhere to be seen.

Carol's immediate reaction was, "Boy-oh-boy, Cathy, we can really play a lot of games now. Let's hurry to the games room."

But Cathy insisted upon first looking into all the stores along both sides of the mall to see if they could find the man. But it was no use; some of the stores were quite crowded, not even Cathy had paid much attention to him, and he had been walking away from them while Cathy was keeping her eyes on that little piece of paper.

All this time they kept arguing back and forth:

"Carol, that man must have dropped the money when he got out of his car."

"Come on, Cathy, 'losers weepers, finders keepers' is what my dad says."

"But the man might need that money to buy food for his family."

"Oh, come on, he's got a nice shiny new car; what's more, you didn't really see him drop it."

"Well, maybe not, but it sure looked like it fell away from him when he got out of his car."

"But you're not sure, so let's come back to the mall again tomorrow; we don't have much time to play now."

"I don't know; my family always says that if you find something, you should try to locate the owner before you figure it's yours to keep.

Finally, even Cathy was willing to give up the search. Carol had become highly impatient, so they went on to the video-games room. The little remaining time passed quickly as they played several games. Cathy didn't enjoy them as she always had before, and she was glad that their time ran out before the twenty-dollar bill had to be broken.

Carol's mother was waiting for them when they got back to the car. Cathy asked her, "Mrs. Marks, can you wait a minute, please, 'til I write a note?"

Mrs. Marks answered, "Of course, Cathy, but why do you need to write a note right now?"

"I found twenty dollars," Cathy told her, "and I think it belongs to the man who got out of that blue car over there."

As Cathy took a page from one of her notebooks, Carol said to her mother, "She doesn't know for sure that the man dropped it. Shouldn't she keep it?"

Mrs. Marks repeated what Carol had said was her father's saying, "Well, you know we always say 'losers weepers, finders keepers.' That teaches you to take care of your things."

Cathy wrote, "If you lost something here, call 698-7243." She put the note under the windshield-wiper on the driver's side, and they left for home.

"Cathy," her friend complained, "why did you have to do that when we could have had such a good time tomorrow in the video-games room?"

Cathy's reply was, "Well, if the man doesn't call, or if he can't tell me what I found, then I'll feel all right about keeping the money. But if he can tell me that it was twenty dollars he lost on the parking lot, then I'll return it to him. I'm sure that's what my mom and dad would want me to do."

Carol's mother had one more comment as she stopped the car to let Cathy out at her house: "Cathy, you'll never make it in this world giving away what's rightfully yours."

The Law

The case law of most states deals with persons' rights to lost or abandoned property which they may find. Those rights have developed over a long period of time and are generally determined by whether such property is truly "lost" or "abandoned," whether the owner of the property can be identified.

If the owner of the property can be identified, or if the owner can clearly identify the property, it is not "lost" or "abandoned" and the person who finds the property may not keep it. For example, a wallet found in a parking lot is easily identified by its contents and it, and its contents, are not lost. One who finds such things has no right to keep them.

But if the property cannot be identified, or if its owner cannot be located, the person who finds it may keep it. A radio found on the beach with no people around has probably been lost by its owner. Should someone find it, he could probably keep it.

Discussion Questions

1. This case presents a moral or ethical problem, as well as a legal one; it's a matter of values as much as a matter of law; how are laws and values related?
2. Is the amount here an important consideration? Does it matter whether it's $1 or $20 or $100?
3. Should the need of the loser affect the finder's decision on what to do? Does it make any difference whether the loser is rich or poor?
4. Do you share Cathy's values in this case or Carol's?
5. Would it make any difference in what you'd do whether you were alone or with a friend (whose opinion of you was important)? Whether adults knew what you'd found?

16 *The Right Punishment*

Alan was talking with his friends before school started about what he'd seen on the TV news the night before. Their fourth-grade teacher Ms. Brooks joined in their conversation, asking what they were talking about.

"I was watching television with my father last night," Alan repeated. "The reporter told about a robber who had shot and killed another man in his store. He was found guilty of first-degree murder by the jury and the judge sentenced him to be executed in the electric chair."

Alan had asked his father what that story was all about.

"Well, son," his father had explained, "all crimes—all bad acts—must be punished, if the person who committed the crime is arrested and found guilty after a fair trial. In the most serious cases the trial is by jury, which means that twelve citizens, after seeing all the evidence and listening to all the arguments, decide whether the person is innocent or guilty. Each side had a lawyer to make the best argument that can be made for his side, and a judge sees to it that the law and proper trial procedure are followed."

Alan's father went on to explain, "There are crimes against property and crimes against persons that occur. These crimes are punished by fines or prison sentences or both. The most serious crime, of course, is murder. A person found guilty of murdering another person may be put to death as the punishment in most states. That is called capital punishment. The basic reason for it is to make the penalty so severe that people will fear to commit that crime."

"But, Dad," Alan had asked, "aren't all those other people guilty of murder too, then? You know, like you said, the jury and the judge and the lawyer and the people at the prison who actually electrocute the murderer? After all, they're killing somebody too."

"No," his father had replied, "in war soldiers kill the enemies of their country; that's terrible, we might all agree, but it's not the crime of murder. In the same way, the police may sometimes have to kill a person who is committing a violent crime, like a bank robbery, and may be shooting at the police or the bank guards or threatening innocent people. That isn't murder either. The police are there to protect all the people from the enemies of society, just as we have to have soldiers to protect us from the enemies of our country. And in a murder trial like this, the jury and others aren't guilty of murder if they decide that capital punishment is to be used, because they're acting to protect society."

Alan had mostly understood what his father had said to him, and he had to agree with most of it. But he still wondered, in talking to Ms. Brooks and his classmates now, whether capital punishment were not too severe and cruel, especially since some murderers are never caught, and there was also some chance that a person might be found guilty when in fact he was innocent.

After school had started, Ms. Brooks reviewed briefly what they had been discussing earlier. All the members of her class were interested in the topic, and they all had quite strong opinions about the rights and wrongs of capital punishment, being about equally divided.

Ms. Brooks then suggested that they all learn more about the subject, making it the topic for "Current Events" for the rest of the week. They might all, she directed, bring in similar cases from the radio and TV news and newspaper clippings. She set up several committees to examine their Social Studies textbook and library references for information on what the law provides. They were all urged to ask their parents and other adults, in order to determine community opinion.

After they knew more, she added, they might invite some visitors to their class—for example, a policeman and a lawyer—to share their experiences. They might also arrange some field trips, such as to the police station and county jail, to get some first-hand experiences of their own. They might even be able to observe a trial at the courthouse, to see for themselves how the question of guilt or innocence is answered.

"What you may find," Ms. Brooks concluded, "is that this problem is just like so many others: the more you know about it, the harder it is to have a simple opinion."

The Law

In one state, the criminal statute limits capital punishment to aggravated murder:

> Whoever is convicted of, pleads guilty to, or pleads no contest and is found guilty of, aggravated murder shall suffer death or be imprisoned for life . . .

Aggravated murder is defined as follows:

> No person shall purposely, and with prior calculation and design, cause the death of another. No person shall purposely cause the death of another while committing or attempting to commit, or while fleeing immediately after committing or attempting to commit kidnapping, rape, aggravated arson or arson, aggravated robbery or robbery, aggravated burglary or burglary, or escape.

Discussion Questions

1. Does your state practice capital punishment?
2. If so, for what crimes does your state allow capital punishment?
3. Do you think the reason for capital punishment that Alan's father told him is a sound reason?
4. What other reasons for using capital punishment can you think of?
5. Can you think of any reasons why there should not be capital punishment?
6. What do you think should be done with people who commit serious crimes?
7. If you were on the jury for a murder trial, would you vote for capital punishment?
8. If you were in Ms. Brooks' class, what areas of the law (in addition to those treated in this book) would you like to study?

Appendixes

Glossary

Abandoned Property. Property which the owner has meant to give up and which he does not want to get back.

Adoption. The statutory process by which a person takes custody of another person's child as if the child were his own.

Appeal. The process by which the decision of a lower court is taken to a higher court for review for possible errors made by the lower court.

Assault. An act by one person which threatens to injure another person and which the other person fears will result in injury.

Attractive Nuisance. A dangerous condition created by a person which attracts children who cannot realize the danger.

Bail. Money paid to a court by a person to ensure the later appearance of that person in court.

Battery. The act of one person's striking or causing injury to another person; it is a completed assault.

Burden of Proof. The duty of a person to prove his claim in court; also the amount of proof a person must give.

Child Abuse. Any act by a person which injures a child or threatens a child's health or well being.

Civil Action. A lawsuit between private parties in court to remedy some disagreement or liability between them which is not a crime.

Common Law. Principles and rules of law developed over time from court decisions and not laws passed by legislatures.

Constitution. The written document which is the statement of the basic laws and basic principles upon which the federal or state government and laws are based.

Contract. An agreement or promise between persons to do a particular thing for a price or benefit to each.

Crime. An act which is a wrong against society as determined by statutory law which is punishable by death, imprisonment, or fine.

Custody. Having complete possession and control of a person or thing.

Defendant. A person against whom a claim or action is brought in court.

Delinquent Minor. A child under age 18 who has committed a crime or whose behavior is uncontrollable.

Disturbing the Peace. An act which interrupts the peace, quiet and good order of the community.

Dissolution. The termination of marriage by agreement between man and wife.

Divorce. The termination of the marriage of a man and wife only for certain specific reasons.

Due Process. The procedures designed to ensure the constitutional or other rights of persons to a fair and just proceeding.

Enforcement. To put into effect; to make sure that persons obey laws.

Estate. All the property a person has, whether real property or personal property.

Evidence. Proof offered in a trial to prove a fact.

Felony. A serious crime punished by more serious penalties such as imprisonment or death.

Grand Jury. A jury of persons to hear evidence to determine if a person should be charged with a crime.

Guardian. One person who is given the care, custody, and control of another person or their property, because of the other person's age or disability.

Habeas Corpus. A request by a person to be brought before a judge, usually to be released from imprisonment.

Hearing. A proceeding, usually in court, between parties to present evidence on an issue.

In Loco Parentis. The legal provision that another person or persons may act in place of a minor's parents.

Juvenile Court. A special court which deals with delinquent and neglected minors.

Legislature. The body of persons at the federal, state or local level which meets to write and adopt the statutory law for their level of government.

Liability. A general term for a responsibility or obligation.

Lien. A charge against property to satisfy some liability.

Misdemeanor. A less serious crime, which is not a felony, punished only by a fine or short imprisonment.

Neglected Minor. A child under age 18 who is not properly cared for by its parents or guardian.

79

Negligence. The lack of ordinary care, or failure to exercise ordinary care; it is a failure to do what a reasonable and prudent person would ordinarily do under the circumstances of a situation, or would not do under the circumstances of a situation, to prevent injury or damage to another person or to a thing.

Ordinance. A statutory law usually passed by a city or village council.

Personal Property. A person's movable property; anything owned by a person except land or the buildings on it.

Petit Jury. A jury of persons who hear evidence in a trial to determine facts or guilt.

Plaintiff. A person who brings a claim or action against another person in court.

Real Property. A person's property which is land or the buildings on it.

Shoplifting. Taking goods from a store without paying for them.

Statute. A law passed by a legislature.

Subpoena. A written order from a court to a person for that person to appear in court.

Summons. A written notice from a court to a person to inform that person of a lawsuit filed against him and to require that person to answer the claims.

Tort. A general term for any wrong act by one person against another resulting in some injury or damage to the other person.

Trespass. Generally, a wrongful act, such as a tort; specifically, it is entering onto the land or property of another person without consent.

Vandalism. Destruction of property without thought or care for its value.

Violation. The act of breaking a legal rule, obligation or responsibility.

A Mock Trial Exercise

Suggested number of persons for exercise:
  1 - Judge
  1 - Plaintiff
  1 - Plaintiff's Attorney
  1 - Defendant
  1 - Defendant's Attorney
  2 - Witnesses
  1 - Bailiff
  6 - Jurors (to be selected from group)

Optional props: Black robe and gavel for Judge
                Bible for Bailiff

The room in which the trial is to be held should be set up like this:

	Judge's Desk
Bailiff's	Witness
Desk	Chair

Jury
Seats

Defendant   Plaintiff
and Attorney   and Attorney

Observers and witnesses

The trial should proceed as follows:

Court called to order by Bailiff.

Judge instructs Bailiff to call Jurors to be seated and questioned by attorneys.

Jury selection — call jurors by drawing lots; attorneys may question about ability to fairly weigh the evidence and make a decision according to the law.

Judge instructs attorneys to make opening statements.

Opening statements by attorneys — each attorney, beginning with Plaintiff's attorney, makes a brief statement of what they will prove.

Plaintiff's case — Plaintiff testifies; Witness #1 testifies.

Defendant's case — Defendant testifies; Witness #2 testifies.

Judge's statement of the law.

Jury considers case and announces decision.

General Instructions:

Bailiff calls court to order by stating: "All rise; this court is now in session, the Honorable ________ Judge, presiding."

Bailiff swears in all witnesses, including Plaintiff and Defendant, by having them place their left hand on a Bible, raising their right hand, and stating the following: "Do you swear the testimony you give will be the truth, the whole truth and nothing but the truth, so help you God?" The witness should answer: "I do."

When the jury retires to consider the case, the Jurors should choose a foreman (chairman) to count their votes and read their decision to the court. The Jurors must all agree on their decision.

The attorneys will need to form a few questions, based upon the testimony to be given by their witnesses, to ask each witness. They each will question, or cross-examine, the other side's witnesses and their questions should attempt to get unfavorable information from that witness.

Plaintiff's testimony is based on the following:

On February 15, Plaintiff was finishing his evening jog and was running up his street, a private street in a subdivision. He was dresssed in his plain navy blue jogging suit. It was sunset. Plaintiff was running at the edge of the right hand lane with traffic to his back. There were no sidewalks.

Plaintiff suddenly heard the sound of a car approaching him from behind. He saw no headlights, but as he heard the car get closer he turned, saw the car just about to hit him and that is the last he remembers until he awoke in the hospital four days later.

He was in the hospital three weeks and could not go back to work until seven weeks after the accident. His hospital and doctor bills totalled $7,000.00. Because he could not work he was not paid for seven weeks and lost $3,500.00 in pay. Plaintiff was in a great deal of pain while in the hospital and, because of an injury to his knee, will have a slight limp the rest of his life.

The testimony of Witness #1 is based on the following:

On February 15, Witness, Plaintiff's next door neighbor, was taking his trash to the curb when Plaintiff went jogging past and waved and said hello. Plaintiff was jogging with traffic along the edge of the street.

Witness turned to go back into his house and had walked back, half way up his driveway, when he heard a car round the corner. The car did not stop for the stop sign at the corner and sounded like it was going fast. Witness turned back toward the street in time to see the car, which he recognized as Defendant's, a neighbor down the street, speeding toward Plaintiff.

Defendant's car struck Plaintiff knocking him into the air and down the street some 20 feet. Witness ran to his house and called an ambulance then ran back outside to see how Plaintiff was. When Witness reached Plaintiff, Witness #2 and Defendant were bending over Plaintiff who was lying unconscious in the street with his head bleeding and his leg bent in a funny way. Very soon the ambulance arrived and took Plaintiff to the hospital.

Defendant's testimony is based on the following:

On February 15, Defendant, an 85 year old person, had gone to the drug store to have a prescription filled. His secretary usually drove him but was off for the day. Defendant wears glasses but does not like it to be known that he has a glass eye. Defendant does not like to drive at night so he was in a hurry to get home before it got too dark.

As Defendant approached his street he only slowed at the stop sign at the corner because that is what everyone does anyway. He speeded up as he rounded the corner and started up the street.

Suddenly he saw a dark something or someone in the right-hand lane but he could not see it well because it was dark. He was not able to stop before hitting the object. As soon as he stopped he jumped out of the car and saw Plaintiff lying in the street.

He noticed a headlight was broken on his car but he had not noticed it before then and assumed it was broken when he hit Plaintiff. It cost $450.00 to repair the damage done to Defendant's car as a result of hitting Plaintiff.

The testimony of Witness #2 is based on the following:

On February 15, Witness had been to the grocery store and was returning home in his car. It was nearly dark when, driving on a street near his home, Witness suddenly saw Plaintiff in his headlights. Plaintiff was dressed in dark clothes and it was difficult to see him.

Witness swerved quickly and avoided hitting Plaintiff, but honked at him. Witness lived a couple of houses from Plaintiff and knew Plaintiff would be jogging home shortly. Witness decided to park his car in his drive and to warn Plaintiff about jogging on the wrong side of the street and about wearing more visible clothes.

As he pulled his car to a stop in his driveway and opened the door, he heard a scream and a loud thump. He ran to the street and saw Plaintiff lying in the street in the light of Defendant's car. Defendant was getting out of his car and running to Plaintiff saying, "I couldn't see him until too late!"

Plaintiff was unconscious and his head was bleeding and his leg was bent in a funny way. Very soon the ambulance arrived and took Plaintiff to the hospital.

The Judge's statement of the law to the jury should be as follows:

Negligence is the want (lack) of ordinary care by one person which causes damage or injury to another person. It is doing something which one should not do under the circumstances, or the failure to do something which one should do under the circumstances. You may think of it as carelessness, which may not be excused, that causes a loss to someone.

When one person is negligent toward another person and causes them damage or injury, the negligent party is liable to the other person for all damages or costs which result from the negligence. These damages may include the cost of medical treatment, lost income, and a sum of money for the pain and suffering experienced by the injured person and for any permanent or long lasting effect of an injury.

In this state, however, if any negligent act by the injured person contributes to, or helps cause, his injury, we compare the negligence of both parties. If the negligence of the injured person is greater than the other person, the injured person cannot recover anything. If the negligence of the injured person is not greater than the other person, the amount the injured person can recover as damages or costs is reduced by an amount equal to his share of negligence.

For example, *person A* negligently injures *person B* causing B $1,000.00 damages. But B is also negligent, in part, causing his own injury. It is found that B is one-fourth (25%) negligent. A is liable to B for only three-fourths (75%) of B's damage, or $750.00, because we reduce B's damages by an amount equal to B's share of the negligence, or $250.00.

So you, the jury, must decide first if Defendant was negligent toward Plaintiff. If not, that is all you must decide. If you do find Defendant negligent, you must decide the amount of damages Defendant owes Plaintiff.

Then, you must decide if Plaintiff was also negligent. If not, that is all you must decide. If you do find Plaintiff also negligent, you must decide his share of negligence. If Plaintiff was more negligent than Defendant, that is all you must decide because Plaintiff may not recover. If Plaintiff is less negligent, you must finally determine the amount by which Plaintiff's damages must be reduced.